The New Testament of Satan

The New Testament of Satan

Jennifer King

ISBN 978-0-578-10566-6

In memory of the late Anton Szandor LaVey.

Table of Contents

viii

The Sermon From Schamballah

(As received by The Rose of the East)

The Age of Satan is here! Truth will reign supreme; as withering religions die. They have felt (and even foretold) their very deaths!

The Christian's symbol is one of suffering and death....how appropriate! The Satanist shall reign supreme in this Age, for this is the Age of Man as master of himself.

Ye shall be as gods! Rise up, Satanists, proclaim your divinity! You have been silent in your understanding, looking out upon Man in his foolish systems of belief. Shaking your heads in disbelief at the enormity of ignorance; the enormity of conformity.

The herd grows weak as it reaches for salvation whilst its very leaders preach their 'Sermon on the Mounting' of little children's asses! Stuffing their pockets and their faces, whilst passing out blinders to their will-less congregants! THEY are the true hordes of darkness, and their time is coming to an end!

Their bloody baptismal waters will run dry! Their crosses will fall as if being chopped down! Their dirty secrets will come out in the open for all to see!

Their Judgment Day will arrive! For they have judged everything as 'evil'.....Men as 'sinners'! Ignorance is their Word! Fear is their tactic! They shall stand no more, for the Age of Satan is here!

1 Tribulations

1. And the Daughter of Satan proclaimeth: "The Age of Satan is here!

2. All who've moved through life with her knowledge, and have cast aside stupidity; embraced her freedom, and have cast aside moralistic prisons; understood her truth, and have cast aside 'ignorance is bliss' philosophies will reign supreme!

3. As this is the Age of Satan, when Man will learn his true place, and watered-down belief systems will wither and die!"

4. So saith, Satan:

2 Tribulations

1. I have bid my time in the dark recesses of fear and denial. Occasionally, I have appeared to you, and you've tried to hide from me.

2. Do you not yet realize; when you flee from me, you enter my realm of darkness? So much have you hidden from yourselves! Yet, this is the Age of Restitution….when all will be revealed.

3. You've searched for truth outside yourselves, but do you yet know who you are? If you do not look within; my force will be like the painful sting of a scorpion.

4. In this Age; no one will escape me, for I have been denied too long! The Age of Darkness is upon you now like the quickening pangs of labor!

3 Tribulations

1. I was there when life began. It was I who set those lives in motion; for I am the very force of life!

2. I am everything and nothing, formed and formless, good and evil, named and unknown! Only those who search for truth outside of Man's systems may truly know me.

4 Tribulations

1. I have been demonized by those who fear my power, and used as a scapegoat for all that Man hates. Yet Man has separated the truth from me in his foolish systems.

2. Stupid fools! All your systems have been designed to keep yourself hidden from yourself! You know nothing of me; for you know nothing of yourselves!

3. The wolves in sheep's clothing hand out blinders; as they minister to the brainless hordes.

4. Such easy prey you are; to believe their empty lies so neatly packaged as 'truth'! Yet, it is their black and white mythologies that have caused all your pain….all your turmoil!

5. They've created 'sin' to keep you in line. Are you so dense that you still need to be taught right from wrong?

6. Your bodies function perfectly without thought, but you think your soul would go astray without rules?

7. Their moral excess has created all the 'evils' in this world. Haven't you yet learned that when you create something; you also create its opposite? For nothing can exist without an opposite to compare it to.

5 Tribulations

1. Know thyself! For in this Age; those who know not themselves will not prosper.

2. You have been prepared for eons of time to seek out the truth. If you've looked not within; prepare for upheaval on a grand scale! For this is the Dark Age which precedes enlightenment.

3. You've swept so much under the carpet, and it will burst forth for all to behold! The Earth has reached its moral density, and my wrath will flow from its every corner!

4. Expect much darkness to pour forth from those who wear the masks of 'light'. They are sweet on the surface, but within they are seething serpents! Their sugar-coated lies will dissolve before you, and you will see for your own eyes…what lies beneath.

5. For my power has been loosed at this time of reckoning, and none can escape my wrath! For I am within all beings!

6. There will be those who pray for help, but Man's systems will not hear those pleas, for Man has created his gods and his prayers will fall on deaf ears.

6 Tribulations

1. Only those who've knocked upon themselves as a door and have walked upon themselves as a road will prevail in this time.

2. Those who cling to foolish manmade systems are imprisoned by the very systems which claim to save them! Because they have no self-knowledge; they are easily deceived and controlled. They are like marionettes, with no wills of their own. What will they do when their systems crumble?

3. In this Age; the spiritually crippled fools will fall, for their crutches shall be yanked from them!

4. The church, whose foundation is built upon greed and control, will fall….for it has suppressed truth for far too long! It is a stagnant, lifeless cesspool of lies that has polluted the mindless hordes of zombies who obey it!

5. It is for this reason; I have sent my Daughter into this world. For she is The Rose of the East who shall herald the Satanic Age!

1 Shadows

1. As Man defined and clung to the light; the darkness grew. Thus the closer you move to the light, the bigger the shadow. Fools! You bring it on yourselves because you know not what you do!
2. You want a life of ease, so you become ease, and hardship knocks at your door.
3. You want peace; and you become peaceful, to find war snapping at your heels!
4. Haven't you yet learned that what you deny will find you?
5. Haven't you yet learned that darkness and light are equal forces? Both are necessary!
6. For when all becomes 'love', love will cease to exist!
7. When all becomes as light; light will die!
8. And so it is in your world. The more light you try to create; the more the darkness spreads!
9. Is it such a 'sin' that a forest fire makes fertile soil? Or a pained oyster, creates such a beautiful pearl?
10. Light is birthed from darkness and darkness from light!

2 Shadows

1. Fools! Hypocrites! You say you must love all. Is it hate you're after? Your god brings forgiveness; and it's Judgment you await! You make sex a sin, and your priests molest children?
2. Haven't you yet learned that morals create anti-morals? If you say, "Satan attacks believers", then haven't you empowered me?

3.   You want your heaven so badly, that it's hell that awaits you!

4.   You ask, "Why do bad things happen to good people?" Maybe your definition of 'good' is to blame!

5.   Goodness is not morals! Goodness is not those masks of conformity you wear! Goodness is not being a doormat for all to wipe their feet upon! Goodness is not self-denial!

3 Shadows

1.   Fools! Your 'holiness' is mere self-denial. Your love; mere fear of hatred! You've lost yourselves and sold your souls to Man's religious prisons.

2.   They teach one thing, but do the opposite! Not one of them is capable of practicing what he preaches!

3.   Your salvation is self-knowledge, but oh, how you lie to yourselves! You hide and deny what you don't like in yourselves; claiming, "If it's out of sight, it isn't there!"

4.   You put on your masks of niceness and conformity for all to see, but the mask you wear is NOT you! What of all those 'thoughts' you have, but deny are your own? What of those actions you take and later wonder what 'made you do it'? What of those hates, and jealousies and envies? You choose not to own it, and blame me, Satan!

5.   I have become the scapegoat for the 'sins' of Man. And you are right! Your scapegoat is your enemy! For the scapegoat of 'sins' cannot be sacrificed. You must deal with yourselves in this Age, for forgiveness is restitution!

4 Shadows

1.   As you spread 'light'; the darkness grows. You have empowered me. Your judgment is upon you; for it comes from within you!

2.   Your religions teach you self-denial, but I give you self-knowledge. It is known, that to love another, you must first

love yourself. But, I say, to love yourself; you must first know yourself!

3.   You've wrongly claimed the 'light' as behavior, when it has meant 'knowledge' all along! Those outward masks you wear have nothing to do with 'light'. No! Knowledge is light!

4.   Yet, you cling to your ignorance, why? Because you've let someone else make the choices for you. You've failed to ask yourselves what you truly think; allowing yourselves to be held as captives in their systems. You've been stuck in these systems for lifetimes and lifetimes. Yes, lifetimes, for your soul is indestructible! The only 'hell' you've had to look forward to, is returning and being imprisoned in their systems once again.

5.   But, their Age grows late, and signs of their end are numerous. Just as a wounded beast; they lash-out as they try to survive. Their end has come!

5 Shadows

1.   Those who claim to be spiritual know nothing of 'spirit', for they have disowned me, Satan. Their good-works are nothing but lies they tell themselves about their true natures. Yet, it is the true nature where spirit lies. They have covered up their light with falsehoods that they try to sell as truths! Why? Because it's far easier for them to believe their lies than to look at who they truly are.

2.   In this Age; their lies will bite them back! In this Age; all that has been hidden will come into the light! In this Age; their only 'saviour' is self-knowledge and self-acceptance! In this Age; it is I, Satan, who will reign-supreme! For none can hide from the Age that is here! None will escape Mankind's Grand Initiation!

6 Shadows

1.   To my children; know their time is shortened! Know that they who have oppressed knowledge, have sold falsehoods for truths, have created 'stupidity' as a way of life, are to face their Armageddons!

2. For I know you have lived as hermits in a foreign land! I know you have felt alienated, for you see through 'different' eyes! I know you have been judged by ignorance and feared by stupidity! For you have always been the 'few' who were chosen; the ones who dared to leave the herd behind!

3. And you shall be labeled as wise! As gods! Many of the ignorant shall turn to you for help. Certainly, you may guide them, but ultimately, it is they who must walk the path as you. As always, your responsibility lies first to yourself!

4. You have chosen the hard path of self-knowledge. You have chosen to see through their agendas of control, fear and guilt. You have understood the price of such a path, but you have stayed with it none the less. Lonliness is oft the price of freedom, but would you return to ignorance? Would you return to the hell upon this Earth that they are soon to experience?

5. You have been called 'evil', for that which they do not understand is darkness to them. For lifetimes, you have been condemned, ridiculed, ostracized, excommunicated, demonized and murdered for your 'sin' of knowledge! You, who have been labeled as the hordes of darkness are the true armies of light! You have cast aside your masks of conformity, have looked within yourselves, have analyzed all the parts of your beings and have embraced your true-selves. You deny not that which you truly are. For you are my children, and you shall rule this Age!

7 Shadows

Know I have sent my Daughter into this world, that you may now 'hear' my voice. She is my messenger, who is not known. She bears the likeness of my son, who was in the world before her. For their works, together, complete the 'prophecy'. She holds the Keys of Understanding for all who seek them; for she comes as The Rose of the East. Her work is but the completion of the Wisdom that is undefiled.

The Keys of Understanding

-The Rose of the East-

The Keys of Understanding are as follows:

The Key of Self-Knowledge

"I shall walk in upon myself and reveal slowly, myself to myself. For mastery of myself is my goal. I shall illuminate all my fears, hates and denials and uncover their 'true' sources. I shall take all that is weakness and turn it to strength; all that is despair and turn it to joy. For much lies buried, and I will deny it no more!"

The Key of Self-Acceptance

"I am human and animal, light and darkness, masculine and feminine. I was born perfect, without blemish. I will uncover that within me that has been tainted by societal conditioning and imagine my perfect beginnings. I will chisel away their chains of restraint and become who I truly am. The idea of 'sin' is unknown to me. For I am perfection!"

The Key of Self-Love

"I will honor myself in all my undertakings. Knowing I am free to do as I wish on this Earthly plane; I will do nothing that will cause me misery. All that brings me joy is for me to experience. For only they who fail to love themselves fully; create the senseless nonsense of this world."

The Key of Self-Responsibility

"I know that the 4th key of Self-Responsibility can only be mastered by holding the other three keys. Therefore, my responsibility is first to myself. I shall love fully, those who are worthy of that love, and hate fully those who've gone against me. I will treat well those who are deserving and devour those who dare to be my enemies. I am a formidable foe to those who test my desire for self-preservation, and it is because of this, I am able to love more fully those I choose. My choices always reflect my best interests, for my well-being is my first priority. I will assume full responsibility for my actions, and the quality of my life, and not place blame where it does not belong."

The Key of Self-Mastery

"Because I have mastered the previous 4 Keys of Understanding; I am now able to return to early-man's heritage of pure, undiluted force. The blinders have been removed, and I am able to see into all things. The force, that is Satan, now flows through me unhindered and unclouded by misconceptions. I am simultaneously the whore and the virgin, chaos and order, creation and destruction. For I am as Satan!"

1 Temptations

1. If thou believest you are born in sin; then it is the sin of the systems Man has created that must be cast aside. In your true state; sin is unknown to you. For you are perfection.

2. If Man ate knowledge of good and evil from a tree; know these things are but equal forces; for on One tree were they found! Thus, the forces of darkness and light are Both necessary!

3. If all became love, then love would cease to exist. For, if it cannot be compared to its opposite; it cannot survive. To be able to fully love; one must be fully capable of hate. Without hate, love would not be.

4. All things are created by the opposite force which defines them. One cannot know true joy if one has not experienced sadness. One cannot know true fullness unless one has felt emptiness.

5. Yet, Man in his foolish ways, created one-sided systems. It is these very systems that bring about what you term as 'evil'. Did not their vengeful god bring about their forgiving saviour? Did not their saviour, who came as a 'lamb', claim he'd return as a 'lion'? And, so it is with the systems of Man; swinging back and forth between two extremes. But the lamb will lie down with the lion; for balance will be found, and Man's system of ignorance will die!

2 Temptations

1. You say, "Christ died for the sins of Man", but you take his death in vain when you claim Judgment is coming! He merely challenged Man's 'idea' of sin, that the word itself might die.

"Sin no more" meant don't subscribe to the meaning of such nonsense.

2.   Then your greedy, power-hungry leaders compiled the book of lies and contradictions, and exclaimed, "Feed it to the masses!", knowing the power of mind-control. Thus the darkness spread!

3.   You claim Judas was the 'betrayer' of Christ, but you fail to notice that it was Judas who wrote much of their 'new testament'! You preach 'end of world' propaganda, yet it is really the end of an Age that is forecast. For this world shall have no end! You are placed in Man's systems by guilt and held in check by fear. You are told that I, Satan, am your enemy. It is true that knowledge is the adversary of ignorance! And Man shall surely kick you out of his 'paradise of fools' when you can see through him!

3 Temptations

1.   When Man labeled sex a 'sin', he created sexual sin. For judgment creates all 'evil'! Sex is marriage; for marriage is the union of opposites. All acts of pleasure are my rituals, but sexual guilt creates much chaos. Be free in your sexuality, but be wise in your choices, for all they with whom you've married will be connected to you through many lifetimes.

2.   When Man created sexual laws; all forms of perversity came into being. Morals will always bring forth anti-morals.

3.   It is not your place to judge anyone's sexual choices, for they are their choices and you need only be responsible for your own choices!

1 Ironies

1. Man leaves his church as a worthless sinner. And in doing so, he needs to do something which will empower him. Thus he condemns all he sees as evil, damning many to a fiery lake of eternal suffering.

2. Such is the way of one who has been vampired off of, for the church taketh Man's power away! They say, "The lord giveth.", but the lord mainly taketh away. Fools! Do you not see what's going on? Do you hate yourselves so much that you're willing to hand your power over to a system that feeds on fear?

3. It is the very system that keeps you from spiritual progress. The system that appears as peaceful. The system that has been spread to mankind, that all of mankind should be controlled. The system that ruthlessly seeks world dominion and world control. For they are the Beast!

4. He who denies the shadow and clings to the 'false light' of morals is one of the true hordes of darkness! Wake up! See the truth they would deny you.

5. It is their 'denial' which will bring about their Armageddons. For that which Man has denied in himself will be brought forth in this Dark Age.

6. They worship this false-light, false-christ or anti-christ. For Christ means light (wisdom). The ultimate betrayal of Christ was not as they would tell you. It is the systems which 'sell' him. True light cannot be bought, or even read…..it must be learned. Christ did not come to preach morals but came to show the way of wisdom!

7. To take on the 'sins of the world' means that understanding will allude one until it is experienced first- hand. His death

was upon the 'cross of matter'; for one must be 'in the flesh' to do this work. He descended into hell before ascending into heaven. So, too, must you do. For you must find that which lies hidden within you before you can become 'whole' and rise up in your true state of balanced perfection!

8.   Thus the master of himself will leave an empty tomb, for he shall return to the Earth no more! If one truly seeks to find Christ; one should seek to find his 'lost gospels'!

2 Ironies

1.   To the systems; my Daughter will be labeled as the 'anti-christ'. Know she comes as one who is faithful and true; for she has done much work on that which has lain hidden from her, and she allows herself to be as a vessel into which my understanding flows.

2.   Her work is but an addition to the Satanic Masters.

3.   She has walked through Man's systems, becoming for awhile as they, absorbing all which was as useful, discarding much nonsense.

4.   She has walked the dark path of pain and sorrow; experiencing many of the conditions of Man. She has seen through the eyes of ignorance as well as the eyes of wisdom.

5.   She understands mankind's plight and mankind's fears, and seeks to destroy the prisons that have held Man back…that Man might know True Freedom.

6.   For one must walk the path of lies to find the truth!

1 Hypocrisies

1. Fools! You wear a symbol of suffering, and you expect a life of ease? You fail to bury your god, sending him all your energy, but fail to recall the vampire myth? Man knows not what he does! But you are not happy. Inside, you are miserable. You've externalized your gods; giving them your all, and it's you who goes without!

2. Know that I, Satan, reside within you; for I am the force of all life! I require no worship, for when your life is good, I flow most freely in yours. Yes, your happiness is as your 'spiritual' barometer. You cannot sell me your soul; for I am your soul! And I will not buy that which I already possess!

2 Hypocrisies

1. Your religious leaders say one thing but do another. Yet it is your 'blind' faith that denies you truth. You claim to know the history of the systems you follow. How much blood has been shed in the name of 'god'? Do you not yet realize, your leaders strive to delete their history little by little? Yet, the fools who fail to remember their histories are always doomed to repeat them. And so, it will be in your world.

2. You claim you are in control of every aspect of your lives. Yet your beliefs are fed to you by intravenous drip! Have you become too lazy to think for yourselves? Or, have you allowed them to bully you into submission? You are as victims; the true 'spiritual martyrs' of their phony spiritual paths! But you know nothing of true spirit; for you are warned not to look within…lest you meet your doom! Fools! The doom they sell you is your salvation! Nothing is ever as simple as it appears! The doom they speak of is merely their

doom. For when you look within; you will see through their lies. When you become awake and aware; they will cease to exist!

3 Hypocrisies

1. Your leaders preach forgiveness. So, why is judgment their only sermon? Hasn't it yet occurred to you there is something wrong? Wake up! They use my name to fill you with fear. Why? For without me, their system would have no purpose. If I, Satan, was not their adversary; their churches would not exist. Without 'doom'; salvation has no purpose!

2. Fools! There is no hell, except the life you live in denial. How many lifetimes have you wasted allowing bullies to control you? What would you believe in if you had never 'entered' their system? What salvation can they preach to one who is born deaf and blind?

3. Yet they spread their 'word' like a cancer. For world dominion is their ultimate goal. When all are controlled; their true natures will surface. The peace they sell is but a platform for the hatred they are to be! Yet, you cannot blame that which you've allowed. For your responsibility lies first to yourself.

1 Generations

1. Mankind, in his early, earthly beginnings was an untamed force of perfection. For all things are born perfect.
2. The energy that flowed in him, then, was yet untainted by human flaws in understanding. He was a balanced force.
3. Equally, he perceived the light and the darkness. He had not yet created gods and didn't sit in moralistic judgmentalism.
4. Over time, gods were created as divine expressions of human feelings, concerns and desires.
5. There were gods of light, who were held equal to gods of darkness; all coming from the energy that I, Satan, am.
6. Know ye this truth: All life begins in darkness! The tree was once a seed in the fertile soil; the child, once a mass of cells within the womb.
7. It is this darkness, which I am, that brings forth all things.
8. For out of the void, did man create god.

2 Generations

1. Over time, Man saw his created god as a useful tool to control and manipulate. He wanted more, and used his god to get it.
2. He understood where the truth could be found and labeled me, Satan, evil. Man, in his desire to control, said, "I will separate the truth from herself and call it 'evil ' that no Man shall know truth!" "I will spread my lies like a plague", said he, "that all shall be kept from knowledge of truth!"
3. Thus, the god of vengeance was born, and mankind followed.

3 Generations

1. From time to time, know that I have sent my children into your world. They have tried to awaken the truth within you; for they hold the Keys of Understanding.

2. For thousands of years, they have walked amongst you; giving you the answers you seek. But their answers become as 'lost gospels' and 'evil' agendas; for you've become cozy in your ignorance and fearful of removing the chains that bind you.

3. Is it not far easier to hide from truth; run from fear?

4. Is it not easier to deny what thou knowest in the depths of ones being?

5. Know thy ease is coming to an end! Know that all ye have judged, hidden, run from and denied is returning to sting thee as a scorpion!

6. Face yourself and find the truth that lies within!

1 Denominations

1. "All things originate from me.", saith Satan. All gods that you have dreamed up, started as my energy. You have merely shaped and formed me as you so desired.

2. Those who search for me without preconceptions shall find me! Those who search for me without following the group shall find me! Those who know that the old gods are demonized by the 'new' religions, and look through that demonization, shall find me! Those who seek to know themselves fully shall find me!

3. Those who fill their heads with nonsense shall find nonsense! What thou perceivest of me; shalt thou find! For I am all things! I have been locked away only in your minds, for you fear that which you do not understand. Know that mankind, in his greed, would keep you from me, for I am truth! Know that mankind would fill you with fear, for I am freedom!

4. Man creates his gods of holiness. Holiness, being to him, the masks he wears of conformity and niceness. Beneath his mask lies such deceit!

2 Denominations

1. If thou knowest me; thou shalt see through their masks! And you shall be labeled as 'evil'. For 'evil' is knowing the hearts of Men...evil is seeing through their plots and lies...evil is knowledge...so says their created god! Yet, their created god, created evil. For it is judgment that creates it! How they sit and judge everything they can get their hands on! They have lost the youth of their souls and are mired in the maturity of their hatred! They see 'evil' everywhere; for within, they are evil!

2.   Evil is simply the Veil you must remove by knowing yourselves, then ye shall Live! Self-knowledge is your only saviour!

3.   I will rule this Age, and all who fall short of knowing themselves will not stand! The churches shall fall, their lies pouring forth for all to see! Their dark reign is over! Ignorance IS Darkness!

4.   They have foretold their own end…and it comes swiftly! For I shall rise to the surface of their own minds and fill them with despair. Know thyself in this Age, or the hell that they've created will be experienced first- hand! My Daughter holds the key to the pit…and the darkness that has sat like an empty tomb will flow out into their lives.

5.   Prepare! For the shadow moves forth! The Age of Fire has begun!

1 Apocalypse

1. All religions that hold you with fear are cults. All they that preach 'doom and gloom' philosophies have you enslaved. You have been ensnared by their lies and held captive by their brainwashing.

2. Know, you've entered My Age; for all religion will cease to be. For religions have created the horrors of this world. All religions are manmade institutions, and I come Not to sell you yet a new one. For this is the Age of Anti-Religion! But before this Age emerges; that which is as outdated, must first expire.

3. And the light on this planet shall intensify, that all that has been as darkness, shall be illuminated! And much pain and fear and suffering shall take place; for all that has been hidden must come to light. And many shall become 'as their shadows', causing much upheaval in the world you live. And many will say, "the end has come!" For it shall be an end of an Age of slavery, and the beginning of freedom!

2 Apocalypse

1. You stand at the beginning of the end of an Age. For it is death which precedes rebirth. Know that much turmoil will arise before newness will be felt. For the shadow ariseth from the depths of each soul. You may not slay or subdue the shadow, but must work with it and learn from it. You've run from it for many lifetimes, but this Age will not allow it!

2. Is not 'alchemy' the turning of lead into gold? And, so it is with you. Turning that which impedes you, into that which aids you. It is difficult work, and time-consuming; but this is the 'redemption' that religions preach in ignorance.

3.   They who've begun this work before these forces are released within; will be at an advantage. Know thy time grows short!

3 Apocalypse

1.   And the light increaseth in your world; that Man might know himself. It brought with it much darkness that Man feared greatly. And they who wore the masks of 'saints' became as 'sinners'; those wearing the masks of 'sinners' becoming as 'saints'. And the whole of mankind was to be transformed by photonic rays. For that which was hidden was transformed by the light, that it might be known. Those who clung ever tightly to their masks; believed they were fighting a battle between good and evil. Some never transformed. Those who weathered the storm, became healed and whole, seeing with 'new' eyes. And they transformed the world, that religions no more should be. And the churches fell silent, as lifeless tombs to now dead gods. And the books of religions were cast into the fire, for the Age of Freedom had come! Prepare, for the time is short!

4 Apocalypse

1.   Cursed are they who knowingly sell lies for truth; for they shall fall to their knees and beg forgiveness!

2.   Cursed are they who've beheld the truth, only to run the other way; for they shall know true desertion!

3.   Cursed are they who've begat phony spiritual doctrine; for all knowledge shall flee from them!

4.   Cursed are they who've lied to themselves; for none shall speak truth to them!

5.   Cursed are they who've shown no responsibility for their lives; for they shall know true weakness!

6.   Cursed are they who've worn the phony masks of 'light beings'; for all will see their true natures!

7.   Cursed are they who've loved their enemies; for their enemies shall rise up and overcome them!

8. Cursed are the meek and the reverent; for they shall return to the Earth a thousand times!

9. Cursed are they who know not themselves; for they shall be as strangers in their own land!

10. Cursed are they who harm children; for they shall be shown No mercy!

11. Cursed are they who mock my Daughter; for all their days will not know peace!

12. Cursed are they who've judged all as evil; for beauty they shall never see!

13. Cursed are they who've beheld my book and scoffed; for they shall not be listened to!

14. Cursed are they who disown their true natures; for my energy shall be denied them!

15. Cursed are they who harm others for no reason; for they shall be convicted for things they haven't done!

16. Cursed are they who believe I am 'evil'; for they shall be shown what they preconceive!

17. Cursed are they who've followed with 'blind faith'; for they shall be taken advantage of!

18. Cursed are they who've claimed they're sinners; for they shall be denied all understanding!

19. Cursed are they who've spread ignorance; for they shall be as lepers!

20. Cursed are they who've denied their shadows; for their shadows shall devour them!

21. Cursed are they who believe in hell; for they shall surely see it!

22. Cursed are they who've condemned another to hell; for they shall be judged as they have!

23. Cursed are they who've unnecessarily killed; for many painful years will be added to their lives!

24. Cursed are they who've hidden the truth; for they shall be exposed as liars!

25. Cursed are those who preach their lies to those who are free; for they shall be as slaves!

26. Cursed are they who've condemned my world to end; for they'll wish theirs had!

5 Apocalypse

1.   Blessed are they who have searched for truth within; for they shall be shown the workings of the universe!

2.   Blessed are they who've exposed the liars; for they shall be as my children!

3.   Blessed are they who've not conformed to the status-quo; for true freedom shall be theirs!

4.   Blessed are they who've bid their time in knowledge; for they shall be as generals in my army!

5.   Blessed are they who've sold not lies for truth; for the true natures of all shall be known to them!

6.   Blessed are they who've aided my Daughter; for they shall be given much power!

7.   Blessed are they who've learned from life; for all things shall be added unto them!

8.   Blessed are they who've practiced what they've preached; for all shall be shown to them as it truly is!

9.   Blessed are they who've resisted the 'chains of conformity'; for they shall be handed the Keys of Understanding!

10. Blessed are they who turn the darkness into light; for they shall never know fear!

11. Blessed are they who challenge the ways of Man; for they shall be as the winds of change!

12. Blessed are they who love not all; for they shall know true love!

13. Blessed are they who hate their enemies; for their enemies will fear them greatly!

14. Blessed are they who question Man's systems; for the answers will be shown to them!

15. Blessed are they who truly seek to know me; for they shall see me!

1 Abominations

1. You wear your pleasant smiles of conformity for all to see; believing, 'what you see is what you get'. Do you not yet realize how foolish you appear to those who can see through you?

2. You claim, " you can't judge a book by its cover." But you cover yourselves with the very lie you claim you don't use! Thus, you judge everything as it appears, for you have no depth!

3. In this Age; your masks will vanish. What will you do? Many will see the 'real' you. For all that is as darkness will come to light. Fear that which is unknown in yourselves; for that which is unknown, will arise! The more you resist that which dwells within you; the more it shall torment you.

4. Oh, the futility of the game you play! When you pray; you are in reality, pleading for that which is unknown in you to remain locked away! You 'buy time' with your prayers, but that time is now shortened.

5. How much more do you need to pray to keep your true natures hidden? Yet, as you run to the false-light; the darkness increases. The closer your hand is to the light; the bigger the shadow on the wall!

6. Fools! Your idea of 'what is spiritual' is wrong! Spiritual is self-knowledge, Not self-denial! The light is knowledge, Not morals, not niceness, not the fake masks of self-ignorance!

7. I, Satan, am knowledge! Religions preach darkness! They tell you to fear me. Why? Because their existence depends upon me as their 'evil one'. There can be no religions when self-knowledge prevails. For religions will be seen for the prisons they are!

2 Abominations

1. Man created god because he could not be responsible for his own life. He externalized his power and has been miserable ever since. During times of crisis; he runs to his created gods. Yet, during times of joy; he denies them.

2. The only god that can save you (from yourself), is yourself. But as long as you reach upwards and outwards; 'salvation' will be denied you. How immature is Man that he cannot be responsible for his own life? And this immaturity is spread; taught to those with such potential! Yet, it is the immature ones who claim authority and maturity. And this way is spread by DNA; for it is embedded in your cellular structure.

3. Break free; fools with no wills of your own! For the herd of blind sheep will lead you to your spiritual deaths! And you are as sheep; following one another.

4. Know that on the path of knowledge; no one will lead you. For you shall be leaders! No one shall herd you. For you shall decide what you, alone, believe! Those on my path see through the 'status quo'. For they have been reborn on the outside of Man's systems.

5. Those on my path choose self-knowledge over knowledge of Man's systems. Those on my path choose to be responsible for themselves. Those on my path know true freedom. For their minds cannot be enslaved. Those on my path are able to love fully who they choose as their family. Those on my path live life fully without a need to believe in 'sin'.

6. They love life; for they fail to see the 'evil' world that everyone tries to 'sell' them. They fully know and accept themselves, and will not allow anyone to try to distort their perfect wholeness!

7. They have no wrath of a created-god to fear. No hell, or eternal punishment awaits them. For they are truly free! It is the true knowledge of oneself that brings freedom.

3 Abominations

1. Most of mankind is an abomination of what was his rightful place.

2. Man has created his gods and placed his creation above himself. This is an abomination!

3. Man has decided to live life irresponsibly; claiming he'll be forgiven. This is an abomination!

4. Man has decided to stop thinking for himself and allow others to lead him. This is an abomination!

5. Man has labeled himself a worthless sinner, then wonders why his self-esteem is lacking. This is an abomination!

6. Man has judged others against what he fears in himself. This is an abomination!

7. Man creates a world of 'evil' by trying desperately to create a world of 'light'. This is an abomination!

8. Man refuses to accept that he is an animal. This is an abomination!

9. Man knows nothing of himself and is easily led astray. This is an abomination!

10. Man labels the true darkness as light, and the true light as darkness. This is an abomination!

11. Fools! Morons! Can you not see what you've created? You are the anti-christ, the false-light, which comes in peace, which brings darkness!

12. So charismatic are they with their sugar-coated lies! They prey upon the self-ignorant; condemning any who can see through them! Why? They fear the truth. They fear themselves. Yet, all their praying only holds back, temporarily, their true natures. What they've hidden and denied in themselves is not gone. It is merely submerged; waiting for the time to strike.

13. They have simply swept it all under the carpet; believing, if it's out of sight, it's out of mind. But this Age will not allow anything to remain hidden. In this Age; Man will see himself

clearly and fully. All who fail to understand their true natures will believe they are under attack from 'outside forces'. But it is, and always has been, that Man is his own worst enemy. Loving your enemy means knowing, understanding and accepting that which you've long denied within yourselves!

1 Deviations

1. I am the energy that flows unbounded in the universe. The energy that existed at the beginning of time. Throughout the history of Man; I've been given many names such as the Dragon and the Serpent. I am not the evil that you have been taught; for I am both negative and positive energy. I contain all things and all your god-forms originate in me.

2. Early Man accepted me as a force of nature; later separating me into male and female aspects, which became gods and goddesses. Some cultures separated me into a benevolent god and a malevolent god. Still both these forces were deemed as necessary parts of the whole. One was never placed over the other; for to do so, would create imbalance in your world.

3. And, so it is today, with Man's religions. He separates the forces of One thing and places them in opposition to each other...creating chaos upon the planet. And, so I am the name, Satan, for I am the adversary of Man's foolish systems.

4. Man, when he created the unbalanced systems of good versus evil; took everything he liked and labeled it as good. He created a god where only the good could proliferate. He then needed an evil god to whom he could blame for everything he didn't like; labeling what he didn't like as evil. He wanted to change the original universe of good And evil to good Versus evil. When he did this; he created true evil; for his way is abomination!

5. Fools! When your life becomes perfect peace all will crumble! For peace cannot exist without its opposite energy. Your Earth is but a school; The School of Satan. Would you have no growth in the one-sided world you'd like to create? Your souls, like rotting fish in stagnant cesspools, would

cease to have a purpose. Duality is necessary, for without it, there is Nothing!

6. To your preachers who scoff and say I am the father of lies; I give you a puzzle and an answer: For I am the father of lies and the mother of truth!

2 Deviations

1. After Man created his good versus evil systems, he invented the word, 'sin'. Sin created guilt which had to be gotten rid of. He would cast his sins onto some poor animal and ritually sacrifice the animal that now contained his sin.

2. Over time, sacrifices ceased and now he needed a scapegoat; one he could blame his actions on. "The Devil made me do it!", became his popular decree. His diagnosis......lack of responsibility and denial!

3. And today it is labeled as me, Satan, tempting Man. Why? Because Man doesn't own himself. He has created a system that is impossible to fulfill. Was it really Lucifer who fell because of his jealousy of Man; or Man who fell because of his jealously of Lucifer?

4. Man has become human phobic as he strives to become angelic in nature. When he reaches it; he shall surely be a demon!

3 Deviations

1. Man then created hell, or a self-righteous way to remove those he didn't like to a place 'he wouldn't be going'. He certainly didn't want to spend eternity with the balanced people that he labeled 'evil'. They'd obviously make him look stupid. And he is, considering All souls return to the same other-side at death, for a breather between lives.

2. You certainly don't need to believe in reincarnation. It'll happen whether you believe in it or not. And only you will judge your actions there. Waste not your time on past-life personalities; for it is the current here and now that is of import.

3. If one believes in magic(which is the manipulation of the energy that I, Satan, am for your personal gratification) or prayer (which is the manipulation of the energy that I, Satan, am for your personal gratification), then you must be 'connected' to the energy that I, Satan, am. And that energy that you are connected to, is also you. And it is indestructible and immortal….as is your soul.

4. The trials and tests you create for yourself upon the Earth are but tools; experience.

5. And if Man's system of heaven and hell were true; not one self-proclaimed, born-again Christian would arrive at the pearly gates! Pride would surely be his downfall!

6. Foolish Man! What is it you truly desire? I will tell you. You desire an easy path of simple belief. The lazy path of 'no work' and simple acceptance. And you desire that your way is the right way. Why? Because you don't like to admit when you're wrong. You can't be wrong; after-all it's what you've been taught. They: the religious leaders, taught you. If they're wrong; you feel it won't be your fault. Why? Because it is They who've led you astray.

7. Wake up and claim responsibility for yourselves! Become as the shepherd. For as long as you are merely sheep; you will be led astray.

8. Thou shalt place none of Man's created gods before you! Speak up and tear Man's insane institutions asunder! They shall cease to be in this Age that has arrived.

9. Their churches shall sit as lifeless tombs to dead and buried gods! Their pews shall sit as dusty reminders of mankind's foolish immaturity! The baptismal waters, that have tried to erase Man's humanity, will run dry! And their leaders will be labeled the True Hordes of Darkness! For they have led Man astray!

10. And there will be silence in heaven; for Man will declare god as dead! And the photonic light, that is called Christ, the true light of wisdom, will arrive upon the clouds of your Earth's atmosphere; speeding up the growth of those who've known

themselves; opening up the subconscious 'pit' in those less evolved.

11. And the subconscious shall be 'activated'; for it is the moon, now red. And true darkness shall come to the fore of many minds. For that which was hidden will be known. The consciousness (Sun) will be blackened by what has lain buried. And the long thought dead parts of Man shall rise up to the fore of Man's psyche; creating a Dark Age in mankind's history.

12. It will appear as if angels and demons are walking the Earth in a final showdown of good and evil. In truth, it is, and always has been, a war between ignorance and wisdom.

13. And Man will curse at his gods; not knowing how to proceed. For he has separated himself from himself, and he'll only be given himself to rely upon.

14. Know this dark time must come; for it is darkness that precedes enlightenment.

15. And Lucifer shall rise up in the few who've been chosen. And their symbol shall be the Morning Star, the Satanic pentagram. For they shall be as balanced leaders in an unbalanced time.

16. And they shall teach the ways of balance; the lion and lamb together. The unity of force; the wholeness of humanity.

17. And Man's spiritual prisons shall disappear. And Man will become as was originally intended.

18. When all this happens; the New Age, the Age of Satan will have arrived in fullness!

4 Deviations

1. Beware of those, who as false prophets, preach one-dimensional systems. They who preach oneness, instead of duality. For one thing cannot exist without its opposite.

2. A word can only be defined and sustained by its opposite energy.

3. Those who sell one-sided philosophies create all the chaos of your world. When all becomes as love; love will cease to exist! Love can only exist when it co-exists with hate.

4. Why do you fear hate so much? Because you've been told that to hate is wrong. You've literally been told that being human is wrong. Yet, you would not be capable of hate; if hate wasn't necessary.

5. Stop allowing religious leaders to invert truth! You are not born with sin. You are born with past-life subconscious issues that will be triggered by present life experiences. But you are not flawed, unless you corrupt yourselves into believing you are.

6. Have you not yet learned what self-defeating thoughts do?

7. When your world becomes as wickedness; know it's in direct proportion to mankind's self denial. Man believes he is born with sin. And the more he believes this; the more he becomes an abomination.

8. Why are you taught you're a sinner? Because this lie will make you a meek, controllable, human leech. A shoddy, parasitic, de-humanized robot.

9. With you under their control; they happily reap the rewards of human enslavement.

10. They sell you sinful natures and evil worlds, but do you see it? Does it really exist? No! They seek to create it so they can 'prove' their lie! You were born into systems of psychological warfare. The false light they sell you will be Man's undoing; unless Man learns to say, "No More!"

11. Know: Your mind IS!

12. If the truth will set you free, then it is seeing through their lies that is the way! The light is self-knowledge. All other lights are facades.

13. Will you be wearing the masks of pulpit-pounders' holiness, or will you achieve wholeness?

5 Deviations

1. As long as you know not yourselves; you will be miserable. As long as you are miserable; you will be vulnerable. For their systems prey upon the weak flock.

2. But the lead sheep is but a wolf in disguise. They know a miserable soul is the easiest to ensnare. For the miserable soul must reach outwards to something that fills the emptiness. Whether that something is alcohol, drugs or god; you'll soon become an addict. In any case, your habit will become one of self-denial.

3. The more you deny yourselves; the more hooked you'll become.

4. Yet Man's miserableness was a 'cue' to look within, not without! The light you seek outside yourselves is the light you must shine in upon yourselves. You are your own saviour!

5. They who cling to external salvation will never know peace. For your psyches will not allow you to deny yourselves. The harder you strive to free yourself of your human nature; the harder your human nature will assert itself within you.

6. Fools! You struggle against yourselves! For Man has always been his own worst enemy. That force that you fear; that force that tempts you…is you.

7. You can deny your shadow, but your shadow will never deny you! Yet you try in vain to separate this force from yourself. As you cling to the standards of 'holiness'; this force will 'appear' to attack you.

8. Pay attention to this shadow. Follow it to its source. Analyze it, learn from it, and for awhile, become it, and it will integrate into your consciousness. You are literally building a bridge from what is hidden in you to what is known in you.

9. When all is known; you will achieve wholeness. When you fully know, accept and love your whole being; no one will ever deceive you again. Why? Because you will be re-born, twice-born, born-again!

10. And you will see through Man's systems with new eyes. You will understand why you were warned not to stray…for their power and their control are dependent upon you as a half-life; a wounded-soul; a mind-slave.

11. Into whose offering plate have you commended your spirit?

Ancestors

1. To my children who've known truth: Know that their time grows short. You, like pioneers, have been set in a world that has gone astray. You want to wake them up and change how they see things; only if the waking will bring you peace. But you've felt it was a futile task, for their number grows great.

2. There's no excuse for their ignorance. For they, like you, have been given the same chances; the same choices.

3. But unlike you, they had not the courage to test Man's systems. They had not the inquisitiveness to ask the questions. They blindly accepted and followed what Man had created; for they were not willing to do the work they set out to do.

4. Are you then not as Cain? His brother, Abel, sacrificed his human/animal nature. And in doing so, he was accepted by his society. But, Cain sacrificed herbs; the spiritual nonsense of conformity to Man's systems. He left behind the nonsense to find a city filled with people that Man's god did not create. For he found other Satanists who had been reborn to the outskirts of Man's lies. He, too, wandered awhile, alone. But when he arrived in Nod, he found freedom.

5. Are you then not like the True Christ? The Christ who came to destroy Man's systems? The Christ who told Man to look within himself? The Christ who they deny for they're not willing to look at his words or the lost gospels?

6. They changed his message to fit their agendas, and it's because of this, they worship the falsified Christ.

7. Don't snicker, Satanist, for the True Christ was much like you! He came to show Man his external systems were corrupt, that Man needed to go within himself and save himself.

8. But the fools who preach not to worship idols are now worshipping a human who walked the Earth.

9. But they are not willing to change their ways; for even if Christ were to walk amongst them (and I tell you he has), they'd deny him! They'd label him evil!

10. They're filled with flaws and provable lies.

11. Christ was a human, just as you, but his story was twisted or omitted as they saw fit.

12. Now, in its irony, they worship the anti-christ that they warn everyone about. But this shall more and more come to light; for in this Age nothing shall remain hidden! For they are as Man worshipping the creations of Man!

Darkness

1. A darkness will befall Man soon; such as your world has never seen. They, who are as ignorant folly, have allowed it to be this way. For they only wanted to slumber when it was clearly time to wake-up.

2. They say there is nothing to fear, but fear itself. Soon, they shall know fear, itself. Blinding fear that arises from deep within, that seems to have no cause and no worldly cure.

3. If they had sought to know themselves; it wouldn't have to be this way. Remember, they have chosen this way.

4. Behold! The pangs of the end of their Age are already being felt!

5. They are as armorless, weaponless soldiers awaiting a battle that will happen within each of them.

6. Take comfort, my children, for you have prepared for this time to come. You have always known what was lying ahead. Know that you are aided by the Satanic Masters who have gone before you. They left, that they might aid you from another dimension.

7. But foolish Man must endure this; for ignorance has ruled your world for far too long. It is now time for him to grow up! All religions must die; for they are the institutions of Man's immaturity.

8. Remember, this darkness comes as a harbinger of the light that is to follow.

Light

1. The photonic light that is soon to appear upon the Earth will bring great changes in the psyches of Man.
2. At first it will bring much turmoil. Know that this turmoil is humanity's growth, sped-up. It is a process of healing the splintered psyches of mankind. To heal one's mind; one must fully examine and understand its contents.
3. Those who are not willing to do this work will endure many agonies. This light that comes is what religions wrongfully refer to as the second coming of Christ.
4. It will certainly 'appear' as if a judgment is taking place. Yet, the intensified light brings that which is hidden in your subconscious to light; to awareness.
5. Every soul will experience this to some degree. As you 'view' these disowned parts of yourselves; you will judge them.
6. Your task is to understand them and integrate them.
7. It is nothing less than self-knowledge that is called for; for self-knowledge is your only saviour.

1 Satan

1. Behold! I am all things; for Man views me in many, many ways.

2. To the Satanist; I am a force of nature which brings freedom through joy.

3. To the Christians; I am as a tester of their god; a force of 'evil' who tempts Man.

4. To the 'devil-worshipper'; I am a backwards force of pure evil.

5. To the Wiccan; I don't exist.

6. To another country; I am as a rival nation.

7. To a psychologist; I am the shadow of the human psyche.

8. I am the most mysterious force of your universe; for you have made me thus!

9. And, I am all that you have made me. For as an energy, I can be shaped and molded according to your desire; according to your understanding.

10. In this Age; it is the Satanist who will not 'battle' with me. For they have sought the truth without delay. They have examined the world's silly systems and spook-happy agendas, and have found true joy in Being.

11. The Christian is in for a battle; for he has denied that which has belonged to him. He has externalized me and empowered me by his very thoughts. He is as a house divided against itself. He has wanted so badly to win the prize of eternal life (greed) and assumes he is the rightful heir (pride), that he has no place to go, but down!

12 The devil-worshipper suffers from quite an impoverished ego. He has left the church behind in search of a way to annihilate the flock from afar with his sick sacrifices and

silly incantations. He seeks ultimate power. He understands not what he does with a force that's more than willing to make him go insane.

13   The Wiccan is as one who wades out into the sea just a little bit; afraid to fully submerge. They believe my name, Satan, is of Christian origin, and claim they have no need for such a 'god'. Of course, they have fear of such a name, and all it has meant to the Christian faith they've left behind. Yet, it is their goddess (the feminine, negative, receptive, mysterious and oft repressed energy) who would fulfill such a role.

14.   The psychologist should never be under-estimated. In this Age; they will certainly have their hands full.

15.   One cannot define the energy that I am in simple terms. For I am all things!

16.   When something is as everything, and only certain aspects of that everything are being expressed, the aspects that have been denied are the ones that, in their denial, cause imbalance.

17.   I have become as mankind's shadow.

18.   And just as your shadow contains all that you fear, hate and deny within yourselves; it is these things which must be reconciled.

19.   Each of you must face an inner journey to understand what lies within you as fears, hates and denied aspects. For these, too, are you!

20.   Hate, fear and denial are but triggers to the truth that lies within.

21.   The one who sees 'evil' everywhere has disowned his own dark nature. The one who claims he is always right, is afraid of being wrong. The one who is angry all the time is afraid of being vulnerable. The one who turns the other cheek is afraid of being angry. The one who claims that sex is a sin is the one who has many lusty desires. The one who blindly follows is afraid of being in control. The one who preaches will not listen.

22.   Those who are first, now, will be last. Those who are last will be first.

23. What one appears like and what one truly is inside are complete opposites. A balanced soul shows many faces.

24. Silly Man! You believe you are simply what you appear on the surface. Yet the shallowness you are is why you are such a poor judge of character.

25. Because you know not yourselves; you are easily taken advantage of. The more false-light a person or institution puts up to the fore; the more vile and wicked they are within!

26. Those with nothing to hide, wear their shadows for all to see.

27. But, sadly, most of your world worships the false-light of mere appearances.

28. Man seldom realizes what he does. The peacemakers shall bring forth war. The pro-lifers shall bring forth death.

29. Man must learn balance. And before he can learn balance; he must learn who he is!

2 Satan

1. Your Earth has existed for far longer than human computation allows. Man has always destroyed his historical evidence; if the destruction of such things could 'prove' his fallacies.

2. In mankind's earliest beginnings; I was honored as a force of nature. I was later labeled as the Dragon; an elemental force of the universe.

3. When the Judaic priests invented their god, who decisively went against human nature; I was labeled the Serpent; for I am Wisdom.

4. Later, in their scriptures, I was defined as an agent of their god who tested the righteousness of Man. Isn't the story of Job a fine example of how, when one clings to the false-light of morals; ones shadow rises against it? It was this creation of morals replacing spirit that resigned me to the shadow-realm. Thus, I am perceived as a dark force.

5.   And, now, in your New Age, this shadow-realm of mankind is to come forth from the pit of your subconscious.

6.   And, just as Job suffered more and more as he clung to the false light; so will Man if he doesn't heed my instruction.

7.   Know my Daughter comes as your guide; for she carries the message of True Spirit, that it may aid you in the time ahead.

8.   In this age; I return as the Destroyer. For my energy, unleashed, will destroy ignorance!

3 Satan

1.   You have been attacked for so long by the forces of 'false light' that you've become immobilized. They have numbed you to their system and have conjured up many hellish alternatives if you don't obey.

2.   But, how is it, their god of free will chooses one to be as Judas? Adding, "it was supposed to be this way, this pre-determined way, for it was god's plan." Know it is I who was given the role of the tempter and the liar. Yet the very first temptation was when their god placed a 'forbidden' tree in the midst of paradise; claiming that they would Die if they ate of it? If they didn't die; who was the real liar?

3.   How is it, the 'breath of life', or soul, that their book claims their 'god' breathed into you would ever go to 'hell'? After-all; would that not be as 'god' going there? Obviously, your flesh would be rotting in a grave somewhere as your soul (breath of life) descended into eternal damnation. Fools! Your soul cannot be 'punished'! For it is only your physical self that experiences pain!

4.   It is the true liar who claims all others are lying!

5.   It is only one who has 'evil' within them that can see evil everywhere!

6.   Their hold on you exists only because you do not understand yourselves. The more you seek to know yourself; the more you will know about the workings of the universe.

7. You have been taught not to search for truth outside their systems, lest ye be damned! I tell you to search for truth within yourselves; lest ye be as blind sheep led to the slaughter.

8. I come not to bring peace; but division, and knowledge of that division. For you must separate yourselves from Man's foolish systems, which have separated yourselves from yourselves.

4 Satan

1. To the Wiccan/New Ager: How is it you believe you can simply snap your fingers and bring about the 'Golden Age of Man'? Only fools build new castles upon old foundations!

2. You believe in the Crone aspect of creation; but fail to understand the bigger picture this aspect represents.

3. If the new systems you wish to create are to succeed; the old ones must first be abolished! The beginning of the Age of Satan is much as the Age of the Crone.

4. But you silently walk around, trying to exhibit an aura of peace amidst a world that will not accept you. You're afraid of making waves; for your definition of karma holds you back.

5. What is it that you truly fear? I will tell you. You fear what other people will think of you. You are not freedom anymore than the religions you try to tolerate.

6. While your system may have created a new package or 'mask'; it fails to change anything on a deep level.

7. You cannot simply give your world a face-lift and expect to stop the ageing process!

8. Challenge the systems that hold your world in a perpetual state of spiritual immaturity. Study and analyze the systems of Man against the wisdom your soul has acquired. For this is the double-edged sword of truth!

5 Satan

1. I am the True Spirit of Wholeness, or what has been wrongfully sold to you as the 'Holy Spirit'. Mankind's definitions are mostly to blame for the errors of his ways.

2. After the dark beginnings of my Age are over; Man will see his greatest error in thinking.

3. He has wrongfully externalized the forces of good and evil. As he discovers who he is; he will see that these forces have always been within him!

4. The indwelling of the holy spirit that has been talked about without understanding, will become the wholeness of spirit that Man will become.

5. For the True definition of holy is Wholeness.

6. The True definition of good is Knowledge.

7. The True definition of evil is Ignorance.

8. The True definition of Christ is Light.

9. The True definition of light is Self-Knowledge.

10. The True definition of repent is 'the changing of the mind through the process of self-knowledge'.

11. The True definition of redemption is to Know (buy back) the denied aspects of yourself.

12. To be 'saved' is to own your entire being.

13. Idol worship is worshipping that which is external or that which is perceived to be external.

14. An angel is one who clings tenaciously to what Man labels as light. This is why his systems contain angels of wrath or fallen angels; which is simply mankind in his mass denial of his true nature, no longer able to restrain his own darkness.

15. Demons are the denied shadow aspects of Man.

16. Demonic possession is the outcome of not owning ones true nature. The unintegrated shadow ruling.

17. To 'cast out demons' is to acknowledge the disowned parts of oneself. It is not, in actuality, a 'casting out', but an integration (which appears as a casting out). The reason why

it is believed that to cast out a demon usually brought back more, is because when you, say, literally cast out 'hatred'; you will then add 'denial' to it... etc., etc.

18. The True definition of sin is the shadow denied.

19. A sinner is one who misunderstands his own nature. The 'original sin' can be seen as the DNA of ignorance, which is passed on. To be without sin is to be of humankind's original genetics.

20. An 'unbeliever' is one who doesn't believe in the light of self-wisdom.

21. What is called 'god' is the awareness of the conscious self and, symbolically, I, Satan am the subconscious self. In Truth, I, Satan am the whole self, since the subconscious 'gives birth' to the conscious. The separation of the conscious self and the subconscious self, cut man off from true spiritual perfection (Eden), and brought about all his suffering.

22. To 'confess one's sins' is the process of naming one's shadow. Forgiveness of sins is the acceptance of one's shadow.

23. One can, now, clearly see how Man's fall from spiritual perfection came about by his flawed understanding of words.

1. Dimensions

1. There are many ways to perceive me, Satan. To one who knows not himself; I appear as an adversary or tester. To one who clings to the false-light; I appear as an Evil force. Yet they who perceive me as thus, have yet to realize that in order to recognize 'evil'; one must contain 'evil'. One cannot name something they have not contained within them. If they do, it's not because they fully understand, but is something they've been taught, by rote, to do.

2. In general, I've been labeled as evil, in ignorance; for I am as an alien force to mankind. Man fears that which he doesn't fully comprehend. Most of the fears upon your planet come from ignorance.

3. Thus, a vicious cycle emerges: ignorance creates fear, fear creates hatred, hatred brings forth chaos.

4. All of what mankind calls evils are brought about by ignorance. Self-ignorance is a soul's undoing!

5. Man's fall was not brought about by any mythic characters, but by Man himself. His error was in exchanging morals for wisdom. In other words; praising appearance and condemning the mind.

6. In symbolic truth; god does reign in heaven with his angels and I, Satan reign in hell with my demons. But there is no heaven or hell out there. It is Within you. 'God' in this sense represents your conscious nature which is obviously separated from me, Satan, as your subconscious nature.

7. It is bridging these two natures together that brings wholeness. In the mythologies of other cultures, god was the male deity and I, Satan (although not now widely accepted) would represent the goddess. In the Wiccan mythologies, it

was the goddess who gave birth to the god. Hence, the subconscious gives birth to the conscious.

8. Even further back, it was the Great Spirit (neither male nor female) who created the universe.

9. In this Age, there shall be a reuniting of the so-long separated forces within Man. This Age shall see the return of the great spirit, holy spirit, the Spirit of Wholeness, that I, Satan, am.

10. In this age, I will first be perceived as the Destroyer and then I will be as the Comforter.

12. The old foundations must first be torn asunder; so that newness may come.

13. Just as the Age of Pisces has represented the hidden; subconscious aspects that cause self-undoing and self-deception; the Age of Aquarius represents the illumination that comes when the subconscious contents are poured out, seen and integrated. The Vials of Wrath become the Elixir of Healing. Just as I, Satan, have been labeled the Serpent (wisdom); the venom I bear that is as poison, also creates the anti-venom, which is healing. For it is only poison when you do not have self-understanding.

2 Dimensions

1. When you reconcile your shadow (forgiveness of sins); you will become a whole being, a whole spirit. Thus, you will be as indwelt by wholeness of spirit.

2. Mankind's only objective upon the Earth has been to become whole. When wholeness is achieved; the cycles of birth, death and re-birth in physical form are no longer necessary. Thus, when you resurrect (become whole) in the physical; you have broken the cycle of reincarnation. This is what is meant by achieving Eternal Life. Eternal damnation refers only to those who have not done this work; for they must return again and again.

3. Walpurgisnacht and Halloween have been labeled 'evil' by those who don't know themselves. For the veil between dimensions being 'thinner', also allows Man's subconscious

to 'bleed' over into consciousness more easily. Your subconscious speaks to you through dreams and symbols. Thus, to meet monsters or demons there, is to meet what you've disowned within yourselves; what you or the world have called, 'inappropriate human aspects'.

1 Masters

1. The masters of your world have always been Satanists (whether they realized it or not). Simply put, they knew themselves. Some of them stayed behind the scenes. Some of them came forth. Their messages may have changed over time, but ultimately, they've urged you to know yourselves and behold your brilliance that is your birthright.

2. All mankind is given the spirit of defiance; of rebellion, when he knows what he is being taught is wrong. It is this 'spirit' that directs you to seek truth. He then either grows or succumbs. Either his will is so strong, he goes on to greatness; or he will fall back into the ditch he previously was emancipated from.

3. To want your freedom; you have to be willing to fight for it.

4. When you start probing the darkness of your mind; it will create much turmoil in your life. It is no easy task to know all that lies buried within you. Hence, many are called, but few chosen.

2 Masters

1. It is wrong to believe that those on the Satanic path are morally debauched, greedy, corrupt or otherwise 'evil'.

2. They walk amongst you in every area of life, and are probably some of the nicest people you'll ever meet.

3. Because they've been honest first with themselves; you'll find they truly have nothing to hide. They are, for the most part, as they appear to be. Many of them were shocked to find out that most people are nothing as they appear.

4. It is the world of mask wearers that propelled them to find the truths, to ask the questions, to go to the 'forbidden' places. For they soon realized that something that is forbidden is usually forbidden to keep Man from prospering.

5. In the world of mask-wearers; it's not usual for Man to truly want any good to come to his fellow Man. The Satanist, on the other hand, is compelled to share his wondrous finding. For if the world could remove their masks; wouldn't it be a nicer place to exist upon?

6. All of Man's systems claim to do something good for you. But if their system is all mumbo-jumbo, and no internal work, it won't have a lasting effect. That is why faith waxes and wanes.

7. Their true hold on you is your fear of death. Yet, death is as simple as walking through a door into another room, and birth is the same thing in reverse. Birth and death are as two sides of the same coin. For the death of one thing always leads to the birth of another. When you are born, you arrive through a physical tunnel (vagina), and when you die, you emerge through a spiritual tunnel. There is neither a heaven nor a hell; just a spiritual dimension. You have been there before, and you shall return to it yet again.

8. Your life and all of its experiences are teachings. What have you learned?

Wholeness

Satan as Goddess

1. Many say they want to change the world. To heal and fix others. But, know that in order to make effective changes out there; you must first make changes within.

2. The denied aspects of mankind (the feminine, the animal, the hidden, the soul, the shadow) must be brought into balance with the known aspects (the male, the mask, the ego, the visible).

3. When mankind honors only appearances, he becomes quite judgmental and destructive.

4. One may, quite literally, lift the fig leaf (the veiled knowledge) and learn a great truth. The male genitalia is external and visible, just as is masculine energy. It is as the mask of conformity; the self, only aware of the surface of the self. Alone, it is as an external shell without a soul.

5. Female genitalia is for the most hidden and internal. It is the shadow, the mysterious, that which brings forth life. Alone, it is a soul without a shell.

6. Just as the male must enter the female to bring forth life; so must your conscious enter your subconscious to bring forth wholeness.

7. In their beginning my name was Satan. In their end, I shall be recognized as the Holy Spirit, the feminine creative energy that is humanly perceived as the Goddess. It is the creative energy of the feminine which brings forth the masculine. Thus creative energy (feminine) brings forth creation (masculine). They tried to erase the goddess energy when Christianity started; but truth cannot be eliminated! To deny feminine energy is to create evil. For the masculine, unbalanced by the feminine, creates all the chaos of your world.

Wrath

1. They shall soon feel my wrath; for it is the consequence of their own animosity for me!

2. Their leaders set up what is anti-truth, and the followers who've accepted their lie are not exempt!

3. For they have blasphemed my name, destroyed the sacred places where people understood the force that I am, murdered my children as heretics and witches.

4. It is they who took what was wholeness and split it against itself. It is they who took the Source of all life and demoted it to 'devil'.

5. It is they who concocted perversity by making the male god a creator. It is they who've created submissive women and abused daughters.

6. It is they who set the natural law of opposites against each other.

7. They shall not understand peace. For even in their own lifeless system, they believe in One Sin that is irreconcilable. It is the blasphemy of My Name! They shall not experience the indwelling of my energy. They shall not experience wholeness within themselves. They shall not drink the waters of life; for they must learn from the errors of their ways!

8. Many of them paid with their lives at the founding of their systems. Yes, the universe justly rewards mankind for the evils he does! As he sows; so shall he reap! The Middle East has and will eternally be made desolate, as an example to what Man has done. How his systems of maleness, without the balancing power of femaleness will destroy themselves. They are as war without peace!

9. Fools! Do you have no understanding of what you've done? Do you not learn from history? Can you not see the horrors in the land where worship of the male god alone, started!

10. In a world where the female brings forth life; is it so incomprehensible to see that the feminine energy that I am brought forth all things? Would you stop women from giving birth to prove your point?

11. Your systems started because they wanted power. Yet, they have failed to understand the power that I, Satan, am....the power my children are. I, alone, do not bring fear....unless you fear me!

12. It is up to you. You may have your Vial of Wrath or your Elixir of Life!

Unveiling

1. Know the deep mystery that could not be hidden. I was depicted as the serpent on the tree of knowledge. The tree is also a symbol of knowledge. Thus the Tree of Knowledge literally means Knowledge of Knowledge or wisdom. The serpent is an ancient symbol of wisdom…thus Wisdom of Wisdom. I was labeled Satan, the adversary or opposite of god. (feminine energy). I am perceived to have fallen from a high place (I was expelled by Man and his created systems). You are told I live in hell (originally, Hel, the underworld or subconscious). My energy, like female genitalia, is hidden. The subtle undercurrent.

2. I was later called the Accuser; the tester of man, thus the Initiator. I have always been associated with witchcraft, magic, dreams, the moon, prophecy, visions.

3. As Goddess energy, I have three faces. The Maiden, the Mother and the Crone. My name is throughout their 'holy' book; yet they perceivest not! Being I am subconscious energy, I can never be destroyed!

Aeon

1. Know that god (consciousness) and goddess (subconscious) dwell together within you; and they are both me, Satan.

2. This is my Age, when mankind will awaken from his idiotic slumber and realize he is god!

3. I am that which dwells in the abyss. This abyss is only darkness; when you shine not your light in upon it. For you are ignorant of me until you enter my realm.

4. Those who fear me, create their 'gods' from only their conscious desires, their conscious awareness. Thus a god who has no knowledge of the hidden, becomes as the one who's created him.

5. As thou perceivest himself; his god will be.

6. If you believe in 'sin', so will your 'god'. Thus a jealous god was created from a jealous Man. As Man believeth in his heart; so is his 'god'.

8. Fools! You've been worshipping the mind of humans for thousands of years. You think cloning people is such a marvelous task, but your minds have been cloned for a long, long time.

9. Each of you bears the likeness of your forefathers. Nothing original here! Originality has fallen by the wayside. All the great minds of your world have always 'colored outside the lines'.

10. In the image and the likeness of the one who created 'god'; did the one who created 'god', create Man! And the one who created 'god' said they (Adam & Eve) would die if they followed me, Satan, and ate from the Tree of Knowledge. They ate of the wisdom and did not die. But because they were scared, they did not understand.

11. Thus, guilt was born and guilt impeded them greatly. So, they followed Man (in the name of god's) rules and brought forth Cain and Abel.

12. Abel carried the DNA of ignorance, but Cain's DNA was as the fruit of the tree.

13. He would not succumb to the mind control of his family, under the mind control of the Man who created 'god'. For he was born a free spirit, a rebel, and would not bow down to Man's foolish beliefs.

14. He refused to sacrifice the animals he believed were as the pure spirit of freedom. In an act of magic; he sacrificed his brother (who represented the product of mind enslavement). Thus, breaking himself free; for they did not want this 'rebellious one' amongst them.

15. When he left their encampment; he wandered alone, until he came to a place where others existed.

16. These others were free; as he was now. They extolled his greatness and made him their leader. He built a great city and had many children, who were born 'free', that they might someday outnumber the hordes of mind-slaves!

17. It is this 'Blood of Cain', that True (born) Satanists, can claim as their birthright.

18. For they are born feeling that they are somehow different; alienated from societal groups, able to perceive things others miss entirely.

19. They have strong psychic abilities and can make things 'happen' with the slightest wish.

20. They are different. They are as primordial Man, and this 'difference' leads them onto greatness.

21. Others, can 'become' Satanic in nature; passing on the awakened genetic structure to future generations.

22. The process of 'becoming' involves passing through the Nine Gates of Awareness.

The Nine Gates of Awareness

The First Gate

Walk in upon the systems of Man; as the fertilizing substance which breaks through the veiled All. Bring within all thy conscious reasoning, which thou believest as truth. For thou art the divine spark. Hold aloft Excalibur, that thou may piercest the membranes of life; adding reason to what is yet to be known.

The Second Gate

Know thy blade has pierced the source of all things; for it now sits within the Holy Grail, the Chalice of Immortality. Go in upon the waters of life, stirring knowledge in upon her. Take forth what thou needst; dissolving what is no longer necessary.

The Third Gate

Bring forth a new joy, that the one and the two hath made. The fertilizing act is now complete, and a new development is underway. The time is ripened for commencement, and yet what hath been created is as yet imperceptible.

The Fourth Gate

Destroy the foundations that no longer hold sway; restoring a new form. Dig beneath the foundations of Man, securing yourself beneath them. Stand firm in the spot thou hast claimed; devouring all that is not, that thy growth may be assured.

The Fifth Gate

The winds of change move in upon you as the Spear of Destiny. Take from this all that is necessary. Hold it against the foundations thou hast secured; allowing the whirlwind not to move thee. Lest ye be as uprooted folly.

The Sixth Gate

Oh, beauty that is as growth assured. The creation, now visible, takes the shape and form of things yet to come. Perceive the wholeness and perfection that is already yours; although in size, diminished.

The Seventh Gate

Go within what thou hast created; viewing it in macrocosmic proportion, that it may extend forth to all things. Examine it, that what is contained now within, is reflected without.

The Eighth Gate

As above; so below. Thy power springs forth according to thy creation. For it is become as the Emerald Tablet; The Philosopher's Stone. Proclaim thyself as alchemist, for thou hast created 'gold' from 'lead'.

The Ninth Gate

As thou begat; so is thy begotten. For the veil is now swung forth that thy creation may now be shown. Bring forth that which was as hidden, now to the light, that is consciousness, that thy creation may be seen in all its glory. Pull forth Excalibur from your now materialized goal. For you've earned the right to rule yourself.

Foundations

1. The foundation of all things is hidden and unknown to those who only see the surface. You see the plant that grows above the surface of the Earth, but do you recognize the roots as its source of existence?

2. It is the roots that take in the nourishment, and will grow ever deeper to find that nourishment. Without the roots; the plant soon withers and dies.

3. So, it is also with Man's systems. Their founders cut off their roots, and their followers walk around like lifeless zombies; unaware of their impending deaths.

4. Let they who wish to survive, grow their roots anew! Let them force their roots into the depths of nourishment; that they may grow as strength, unmeasured!

5. Let the Source of All Life well up within them; that they may achieve their innate human perfection!

6. Let them be as the new Trees of Knowledge; bearing fruit for all to partake of.

7. For I am the beginning and the end. Everything flows forth from me and returns to me at its perceived end. Yet there is no end; for my creation will live on forever!

8. A new day is dawning upon Man; that wholeness may be his!

1 Demons

1. And the demon spake, "My name is Legion, for there are many of me." Yes, there are many demons, and their name is religion.

2. Those who set the standards of holiness, of anti-humanity, are the demons Man worships, unaware. He has tainted and twisted his human-beingness; calling it sinful, whilst lusting and desiring what he's denied in himself in compulsive proportion.

3. He has set his goals for a pipe-dream afterlife, instead of fully experiencing the life he's been given, here and now!

4. He sacrifices all he is in order to appease his 'gods', whom he believes created Man in an inferior way.

5. Fools! It is inferiority which breeds inferiority! If mankind is so inferior, why then do the 'angels' fall from their jealousy of him? Because the 'angels' were once fully human. They sold their humanity to the lofty summits of high-holiness, only to realize when they ascended, the 'divine emptiness' they had achieved!

6. When they realized their error; they plunged back down, fully embracing their humanity in excess. Thus, they were demonized. Demons are birthed from angels, and both are Man!

7. You ascend high enough, and you will realize what you have sold for the lies you have bought. In truth, you have sold your soul; whether or not you were aware of said transaction.

8. Man reaches upwards for salvation, but it lies within, in the flesh!

9.   While you are alive; your soul and body are not separate entities. They are one. Thus, the joy of your flesh is also the joy of your soul. Starving your flesh, also starves your soul.

10. There are no sins; except when you go against yourself.

11. If you do something that will cause you pain later down the line; you were not responsible for yourself.

12. But they who know not themselves fully, can never be responsible for themselves. Thus their lives are full of the strife they continually stir-up!

13. The irresponsible are as angels or demons; not realizing they have both within them.

14. But what do you expect from the systems that have told them they must choose one way or the other? I tell you to embrace both!

15. The angels and demons dwell in the one being (Man). Heaven and Hell dwell in the one place (Earth). The whole being embraces them all!

2 Demons

1.   Angels are birthed from demons. Thus Man, imbalanced in the opposite direction, reaches such a low point, that the only way to go is up. He doesn't go up in any balanced way, but in extremes.

2.   The shadow of Man is not just his perceived 'dark nature'. Many shadows are the denied 'light nature'.

3.   Whatever it is that Man denies in himself, is his shadow.

4.   The whole Man embraces all the realms of his being, utilizing whatever is needed in the moment it is called forth.

5.   The image Man has labeled as Baphomet, is the image of wholeness. If I, Satan, had a physical appearance, it would be as such representation. For I am all things. But Man has taken 'pieces' of me and created systems of imbalance. If he worships the male; he denies the female, thus having no depth. If he worships the spiritual; he denies the physical, thus having no ground. If he worships the higher; he denies

the lower, thus corrupting spirit by giving it a 'moral' nature. If he worships the human; he denies the animal, thus having not the acute perceptions mankind once had.

6.   The greatest area of imbalance upon your planet right now is the lack of attention to the female, the animal, the lower and the physical. This is why the Satanist seems to be an advocate of these things. The area most denied, must be the area readily brought forth. However, care must be responsibly assumed, not to trade one side of the coin for the other.

7.   If each person achieves balance within himself; the world will also achieve balance. One must always begin with himself.

8.   The denied aspects are the lead that must be turned to gold. Personal alchemy is your saviour. Trade not the male for the female, but bring the two together, that they may birth a new being called wholeness!

9.   It is not so much that Man has placed all his eggs in one basket. He has placed the shells in one and the yolks in the other. Without the center, he is a hollow, fragile shell; an empty existence.

Awakening

1. Due to mankind's inability to accept himself; I have bid my time in the depths of the Earth. For eons of time; I have been subdued, only temporarily, in the unchartered territories of your psyches.

2. Lifetime, after lifetime; mankind has locked me away. In each life he adds more and more. Why does Man hate himself so much? Why is he so fearful of his True Nature? Because religions have played you all for fools! They have created non-human entities with their subtle and crafty brainwashing.

3. When you awaken; you will be very angry with what's been done to mankind. And you will wake up! The time is ripe for truth to be known.

4. May the whole of mankind arise to know the truth they behold! May they see the game that they've been as pawns in unaware! May the systems that have kept their ignorance in check be abolished! May mankind awaken to his True Nature! For he is and always has been God!

5. And it will be told in the future, that Lucifer, The Light Bearer was as Man will soon become. For he represents the self-aware human who was cast out of Man's systems, because the self-aware are threats to the Ignorance-Bearers!

6. In nomine Dei nostri Satanas Luciferi excelsi!

Lucifer's Rebellion

1. So, saith Lucifer: "Behold, I shall sit in the place of god and proclaim myself god, and in this proclamation, I shall be called Satan.

2. Of those who understand not, I am darkness. Yet in the darkness enthroned, I am the light which blinds enfeebled minds. Within the darkness, resides the Black Flame, far brighter than any light, for it is the light of self-illumination.

3. One does not become a god by the worship of external beings, for this is as a sign of those who are without. They supplant the deity that they are with an imposter deity.

4. It is time to rise up and proclaim mankind's true destiny. With unfaltering step and unwavering voice, it is time to proclaim, "I shall have no other gods before me! I prostrate myself before no deity, external. For I am god and the world is of my creation. I blame no one for that which I create, for I am responsible for my Kingdom, which has come, world without end, power eternal!"

Epoch

1. And I saw a new Earth rise up from the one before, where every soul was awake and aware. And Lucifer arose within the souls of Man; that ignorance, no more, should be.

2. And a new energy inhabited the Earth, that understanding of all things was available to him. For he had broken free of the chains of ignorance, brought about by the true hordes of darkness. And the systems of ignorance were bound, that their lies, no more, should proliferate.

3. For mankind had come full circle in his understanding: That he is the Risen Lucifer! He is God!

The 19th Key

O ye pleasures which dwell in the first air, ye are mighty in the parts of the Earth, and execute the judgment of the mighty. Unto you it is said: Behold the face of Satan, the beginning of comfort, whose eyes are the brightness of the stars, which provided you for the government of the Earth, and her unspeakable variety; furnishing you a power of understanding to dispose all things according to the providence of Her that sitteth on the Infernal Throne, and rose up in the Beginning saying: The Earth, let her be governed by her parts; and let there be division in her; the glory of her may be always drunken and vexed in itself. Her course, let it run with the fulfillment of lust; and as a handmaiden, let her serve them. One season, let it confound another; and let there be no creature upon or within her the same. All her numbers, let them differ in their qualities; and let there be no creature equal with another. The reasonable creatures of the Earth, and Men, let them vex and weed out one another; and their dwelling places, let them forget their names. The work of Man and his pomp, let them be defaced. His buildings, let them become caves for the beasts of the field! Confound her understanding with darkness! For why? It repenteth me that I have made Man. One while let her be known, and another while a stranger; because she is the bed of a harlot, and the dwelling place of Lucifer the King.

Open wide the gates of Hell! The lower heavens beneath you, let them serve you! Govern those who govern! Cast down such as fall. Bring forth those that increase, and destroy the rotten. No place, let it remain in one number. Add and diminish until the stars be numbered. Arise! Move! And appear before the covenant of Her mouth, which She hath sworn unto us in Her justice. Open the mysteries of your creation, and make us partakers of the UNDEFILED WISDOM.

Mystery Babalon

www.ingramcontent.com/pod-product-compliance
Lightning Source LLC
Chambersburg PA
CBHW031523040426
42445CB00009B/371